You
Are
invited
To Be Delighted
in
A Book of Gifts,
Games, inspirations
and surprises

HOW to BE an ARTist

STAY loose. learn to WATCH snails. Plant impossible GARDeNS. invite SomeoNe DaNgerous to teA. MAKe little signs that SAY Yes! and post them All over your House. MAKe Friends with FreeDoM ¿uncertainty. look FoRwARD to DReAMs. cry During Movies. Swing As HiGH As you can on A swingset, By MooNLiGHt. CUHiVATE MOODS. refuse to "Be responsible." Do it For love. TAKe lots oF naps. Give MoNey AWAy. Do it now. the Money will Follow. Believe in MAGic. lAugh A lot. Celebrate every GorGeous MoMent. TAKe MooNBAths. HAVe wild iMAGinings, transforMAtive DreAMs, and perfect CALM. DRAW on the walls. reAD everyDAY. iMAGine yourself MAGic. Giggle with CHILDren. listen to olD People. open up. Dive in. Be Free. Bless yourself. Drive AWAy FeAr. PLAy with everythinG. entertain your inner CHILD. You Are innocent. BuilD A FoRt with Blankets. Get wet. HuG Trees. write love letters.

♥ ©SARK 89

A creative companion

How to free your creative spirit

BY SARK

Celestial
ARTS
Berkeley California

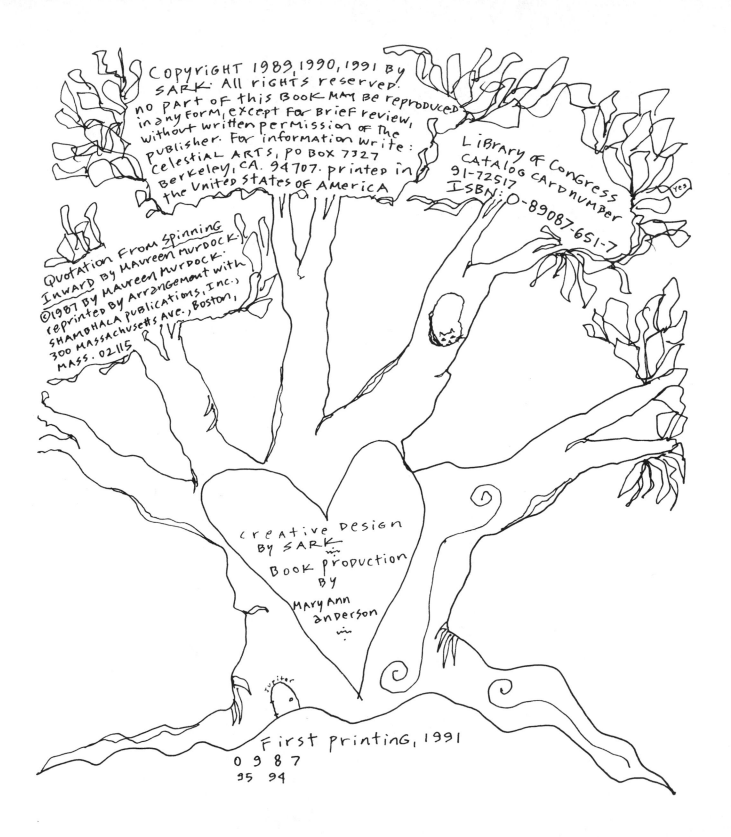
Creative design
by SARK

Book production
by

Mary Ann
Anderson

First printing, 1991
0 9 8 7
95 94

This book is your creative companion.
it will help you re-learn How to free
your creative spirit.
We All started out creatively free.
remember the sandbox? All you
needed was bare toes in warm sand,
and maybe a good bucket.
Then you could build your own world.

At school, things may have changed.
...The chairs were in rows, and
tree trunks were to be colored
Brown, not purple. If you lived
in a world of purple tree trunks,
you probably learned to hide it.

I stood up in my first grade class and said, "Do these chairs have to be in rows? Can we put them in a circle, or sit on the floor?" The answer was no, and I began to hide my creative thinking.

I also began to invent illnesses so I could stay home from school and read, write and create. One year, I missed 92 days! I believe that this saved my creative life.

clear a space for creative thought

You Are already an artist, creative person.
It is GOOD to read this BOOK Lying DOWN, Because that is HOW it WAS written.

THIS is FOR yOU.
Go AHeaD. lie DOWN. yOU HAVE Permission. SHOW these worDs to anyone WHO ASKS,

"Why Are you still in BED?"

reaD. EAT COOKies. WATCH OLD MOVies. Have A BeD picnic.

Y O U   A r e   e n O U G H
Y O U   H a v e   e n O U G H
Y O U   D O   e n O U G H

Robert Fulghum, who wrote:
All I really need to know I learned in kindergarten, touched the place in all of us that wants to nap and play and feel creatively free.

(·‿)

Just for one day:

Hide all the clocks in your house.

Compliment yourself constantly.

Tape a piece of paper over the TV screen and write ideas for brand new shows on it.

Visit every tree near you and spend time memorizing the branches.

Spend $20 on magazines and read them all at once.

repression is poison to creativity. the longer you repress it, the more stuffed down it becomes.

Then you learn the negative self-talk, rationalizing and delaying that prevent creative expression.

"other people are artistic, not me."

"it never looks the way I want."

"I don't have time now."

"anything I write is garbage."

"I may as well just give up."

"I need to earn money first."

"I've waited too long now."

"who cares?"

"I could never sing."

"I can't draw a straight line."

5

To this, I will let Martha Graham reply:

"There is a vitality, a life-force, an energy, a quickening that is translated through you into action. And because there is only one of you in all of time, this expression is unique. And if you block it, it will never exist through any other medium and be lost. The world will not have it. It is not your business to determine how good it is nor how valuable nor how it compares with other expressions.

It is your business to keep it yours clearly and directly, to keep the channel open...whether you choose to take an art class, keep a journal, record your dreams, dance your story or live each day from your own creative source. Above all else, keep the channel open!"

NOW, CHOOSE A WORD or WORDS THAT DESCRIBE YOU, or HOW YOU'D LIKE TO BE DESCRIBED. Or, MAKE UP YOUR OWN.

AMAZING

ECSTATIC

WILD

ENDEARING

BRAVE

TRUTHFUL

ANGELIC

FASCINATING

SENSITIVE

KIND

WISE

FUNNY

RARE

INSIGHTFUL

RADIANT

ENERGETIC

PEACEFUL

STAR-FILLED

CREATIVE

IMAGINATIVE

PIONEERING

BLESSED

BLISSFUL

JOY-FULL

CHARMING

FUNNY

ANGELIC

YES, I KNOW ANGELIC APPEARS TWICE. WE NEED MORE ANGELS!

WHAT DO YOU DO with CREATIVE BLOCKS?

BUILD A castle!

- - - - - - - - - -
YOU DESERVE to FEEL
CREATIVELY FREE

Use this PAGE to write Down a creative iDea or Dream you Have.

Use this page or blank paper to list all the reasons you can't, or haven't yet started living your creative idea or dream. ⌢

List everything. If a thought appears frequently, write it down again. List all details, no matter how small they might seem.

"I can't do it until I clean my closets."

When you have exhausted your negative reservoir, you can rest, and I'll share a story about affirmations.

When I first heard and read about affirmations, they made a lot of sense to me. If we could learn how to replace negative thoughts with positive thoughts, it seemed like we could be a lot happier.

I was swimming in negative thoughts! I began writing affirmations, and saying them out loud:

"I am safe."   "I am rich."

For two years, I thought I was winning the "war on negativity." The problem was, I still had a negative response inside my head to each affirmation.

THen, I learned ABout the "response column."
it works like this:
You write your AFFirMATion on the left HanD side oF A piece oF PAper.

AFFirMATion	response column
it is SAFe to relax	no, it's not!
it is now SAFe to relax	

anD the response to thAT AFFirMATion you HeAr insiDe your HeAD. Mine wAS "no, it's not!" anD thAT Goes on the riGHT.
You keep writing the AFFirMATion anD listing the Different responses. THe iDeA is to work with The AFFirMATion until your minD HAS no response.
In My CASe, it HAppeneD when I ADDeD the worD "now."

THen the AFFiRMATiON is clear, aND is something you can work with.

Turn BACK to the PAGE(s) you wrote your neGAtive thoughts on, aND tear them out of the BOOK.

FinD an empty BAG.

Tear the PAGes into tiny pieces aND put them in this BAG.

Seal the BAG SHut.

Dispose of the BAG.

THis is a useful ritual For "throwing out the GarBAGe" of your MinD. THese thoughts will Be BACK, aND I'll tALK ABout HOW to DeAl with them.

One of my favorite energy-releasing exercises comes from a book called THE CHARISMA BOOK by Doe Lang.

I don't care, you can't make me!
How to do it.

1. Stand with your feet apart. Swing your torso, neck as one unit, first to the right, then to the left.

2. Let your arms begin to swing freely, as your body turns from side to side until they wrap loosely around you at shoulder level.

3. As your body swings from left to right, begin to shout "I don't care!" as loud as you can.

4. Enjoy the sounds. Keep repeating. Add "You can't make me!" repeat 20 times or more.

when I taught my class, "adventures and art with SARK," I would take the kids onto the roof of my building, and we'd do this exercise! I'd see heads peering out of various windows as we flapped our arms and yelled all over the neighborhood, "I don't care! you can't make me!"

I use a lot of tension releasing relaxation exercises in my work, because my mind is intensely active and I am prone to fits of over-sensitivity and crabbiness.

- -

MY MIND IS TOTALLY FREE

HOW TO BE really ALIVE!

Live juicy. STAMP out conformity. STAY in BED All DAY. DreAM OF GYPSY WAGOns. FinD snAils MAKing love. Develop an Astounding Appetite For Books. Drink sunsets. DRAW out your feelings. AMAZe Yourself. Be ridiculous. STOP Worrying. now. iF not now, then when? MAKe Yes Your FAVORite word. MARRY YOURSELF. DrY Your clothes in the sun. eAT MAngoes nAKED. Keep toys in the BATHtub. Spin YOURSelf Dizzy. HAng UPSiDe Down. FOllow A CHilD. celebrAte an old person. SenD A love letter to YOUR SeLF. Be ADVAnceD. TRY enDeARing. invent new WAYS to love. TrAnsForm negAtives. DELiGHT SOMeone. WeAR PAJAMAS to A Drive in MOVie. Allow YOURSELF to Feel rich without Money. Be WHO YOU TRULY ARe and the Money will Follow. Believe in everything. You Are Always on Your Way To A MirAcle.

THE MIRAcle iS YOU

©SARK 90

Begin now, to experience your world in a new creative way.

TRY:

studying something in nature for one hour or longer: snails, ants, butterflies, leaves.

Making a treasure hunt for a friend. Each clue leads to the next, and the clues must relate to literature, art, music, dance.

Taking your child, or a borrowed one, on a "pleasure walk" pointing out everything that delights you.

Having a moonlight picnic.

- - - - - - - - - - - - - -

You are so very special

Katharine Hepburn said in an interview
"Oh, I'm scared all the time! I just act
as if I'm not."

To Live creatively Free:
Do what you know how to do now
then "Act as if" you know how to do
the rest.

I met someone who had been
paralyzed in an accident, and was
told she would never walk again.
She said, "I just acted as if I could
do it, and then I learned how to
embrace the micromovements."
These micromovements led her to
complete recovery.

19

Micromovements Are tiny, tiny steps that move us Forward in some way. Sometimes, when I Feel stuck About WHAT to Do next with A creAtive iDeA, I ASK Myself "WHAT DO I KNOW HOW to DO? WHAT MicroMovement WOULD WorK?"

Sometimes it's As simple As getting the scissors From A Drawer, tAKing out the postAge stAmps, or FinDing A certAin pHone nUMBer.

I cAll this the Beginning/GAtherinG time. It is the most FrAGile For me. I useD to Be the worst procrAstinAtor! I WOULD Get All these BOOKS on the subJect, AnD then oF course, woULDn't reAD them!

My mind moved in great gulps and
I would scare myself to death before
ever beginning. I would leap into
the future.
"How will I ever publish this?"
or defeating "what if" questions
"What if everybody rejects it?"
So often, we are stifled by an
immediate inner censor.
  "Oh, I couldn't do that."
  "That wont ever work."

These thoughts effectively stop us
so we dont even have to try.

          · ᴜᴠ   · ·

I now know that creative thought
is a process that can be learned,
practiced and expanded.

Your Desire to Feel
CreAtively Free
is very important

the rest is eAsY

23

About living creatively free:

I've learned to ask for whatever I want, and trusting that the universe wants me to have it.

One time, I put this ad in a newspaper: "incredible housesitter seeks incredible House."

3 days later, I had a 4 bedroom mansion on Russian Hill in San Francisco. The owner was moving out of state, and wanted someone to live in her house until it sold. As it turned out, I lived there rent-free for 2 years.

Another time, I wanted a job as a reporter for a newspaper, and I called the editor, who said,

"it's too late. we've interviewed everybody and closed the applications."

I replied, "Well, you'D Better open
them BACK up, Because you're Going to
Hire me!"
aND He DiD.
                    .⌣.

Asking, Believing, Visualizing,
Having FAith.
These are steps I practice to HeLp
miracles Happen.
Just remember: money is inciDental.
important, and inciDentaL.
Your Desire and energy are everything.
THATs WHY I say, "Be WHO you truly
Are, and the money will Follow."
            it's true

- - - - - - - - - - - - - - -
you Are Always on your WAY
    to   A   miracle

JUST FOR ONE DAY:

GO on your travels with just one dollar in your pocket. include WALKING, nature, relaxation and SMILING.

THink of an advertisement for something you want, and put it in a newspaper or up on A tree.

Spend two Hours in A library For pleasure only.

Do everything with your least Dominant HanD. iF you Are ambidextrous, Do HandstanDs.

Give people opportunities to BE
Generous.

I just spent 3 weeks on Paradise
Island in the Bahamas, in a private
Villa, thanks to a friend who responded
to my request for a "creative retreat."

We all know people who would love
to help us in some way, and we
can in turn, help them.

There are many ways besides
Having money to help our creative
Dreams to come true. Bartering,
trading, exchange of services are
a few.

T H i n k   c r e a t i v e l y

- - - - - - - - - - - - - - - - - - -

Y o u   A r e   w e l c o m e   e v e r y w h e r e

27

A thought I use for my inner
censors and various negative
judgements:

"You can hang around if you want,
but just remember— I'm bigger
than you are!"

Or an affirmation that was shared
with me:

"Send love to your fears.
Welcome your fears! invite them
in, entertain them, and then send
them home!"

Or a saying by Ruth Gordon:

"Never, never, never, under any
circumstances... face facts!"

- - - - - - - - - - - - - - - - - -
You are now free from all fears
28

playtime / invention

THis is my Favorite part of the creative process.

THere is an Artist in Australia called ken Done. His work is vibrant, splashy and Alive, and it Appears on All sorts of wonderful things: posters, clothing, tennis shoes...
THe world is His canvas.
I found out that He would be in San Francisco, and knew that I must meet Him.
I went to The Department store where He was Appearing, with A Gift for HiM, and my enthusiasm.
I sat on The Floor, reaping A book About His work, and saw

A photograph of him for the first time. I looked up, and he was standing in front of me, chuckling that I was curled up on the floor, enjoying his picture.

During our impromptu meeting, he shared many stories, and this was one of my favorites. He said,

"You've got to MAKE the thing real — whatever it is. This may sound simple, but people dont do it.

Remember, that as an artist, you have visual skills that other people havent yet developed. In other words: They arent able to see what you have VISUALIZED!"

Then he said,

"Here's an example. I had done a painting that I thought would make fabulous sheets — it was bright,

vivid and very free. The sheet
company representative looked at
my painting and said,
"The painting may be wonderful,
but it's very expensive to make sheets
and we're just not sure it would work."

"I could tell that he couldn't see
what I was visualizing, so I went
home, got a big white sheet, and
painted my painting directly onto
the material, thereby MAKING the
thing reAL, and took it BACK to
the sheet company.

A HA! now the sheets could be
made, and they placed a big
order."

- - - - - - - - - - - - - - - - -

let your imAginAtion work for you

This story helped lead me to what I call: A Habit of Completion.

By making the thing real, you then have a "thing" to do something with!

I wanted to make some cards to guide and help people in their spiritual journeys...

So I invented their form.

I tore French rag paper into small squares, and hand colored the edges, then wrote messages on each square. I then folded an envelope out of the same paper, dyed some cotton string to tie it shut with, and wrote a simple instruction guide.

These became Spirit Cards, and I sold/shared over a thousand sets,

MADE in that same FORM. AND it WAS
COMPLETED.

Once you MAKE a thing real, it can
travel without you! You Don't need
to Be there to explain, or to say
"The colors will Be BriGhter "or" it will
Work Better."

While inventing, MAKE it FUN and
SAtisfying to your eye.
PLAy with MAterials! Let any FORM
Be possible.
Breathe Life into your iDEA and
let it COME out of your MinD.

_ _ _ _ _ _ _ _ _ _ _ _ _ _ _ _ _ _

All Great iDEAS need A HUMan
CHannel to bring them Down to eArth

remember to Delight yourself
FIRST
and then others will Be TRULY

DeLiGhteD

I truly thought that procrastination and unfinished projects would Bother Me Forever. Now, instead of A HABit of incomplete iDeAs, I really HAVE A HABit of completion.
WHATever I BeGin, I complete in some WAY, and it is not A Strain AT All. I now see that it is A learned BeHavior—Just As the other was learned.

HOW TO really LOVE A CHILD

Be there. SAY Yes As oFten As possible. let them Bang on pots and pans. iF they're CRABBY, put them in WATer. iF they're unlovABle, love yourseLF. realize HOW important it is to Be A CHiLD. Go to A Movie theatre in your PAJAMAS. reAD BOOKS out loud with Joy. invent pleasures together. reMeMBer HOW really SMAll they Are. Giggle A lot. Surprise them. SAY no when necessARY. TeACH Feelings. HeAL your own inner CHiLD. learn ABout parenting. HUG trees together. MAKe loving SAFe. BAKe A CAKe and eAt it with no HanDS. Go FinD elephants and kiss them. plan to BUiLD A rocketSHip. iMAGine yourseLF MAGIC. MAKe lots oF FORTS with Blankets. let your anGeL FLY. reveAL your own DreAMS. seArcH out the positive. Keep the Gleam in your eye. MAiL letters to GoD. encourAGe silly. plant licorice in your GARDen. open up. Stop Yelling. express your love. A lot. SpeAK KINDLY. Paint their tennis SHoes. HanDle with CAring.

CHiLDren Are MirAculous

♥ @SARK '20

When I was 10 years old, one of my best friends was 80, and his name was Mr. Boggs. He called me his "twirly friend." (Because I did a wheely in his driveway) Mr. Boggs taught me how to play checkers and gave me a microscope. Then He got sick and went into the Hospital.

Everyday, I made him a card, or a poem or did a drawing, and sent these to the Hospital.

Mr. Boggs came home after a month in the Hospital and said to me, "You saved my life. No one else called or wrote, and your mailings gave me the courage to live. Thank you."

I think it was then that I decided to devote my life to being creative.

I HAD A GrandFather who told Me:
"Do everything you can think of Doing,
So you know what you Don't want to Do
For the rest of your Life."
So I HAD 250 Different JOBS From
the Age of 14 until 24.

THese JOBS MADE My Devotion to
creative thinking even More Fierce.

One OF MY FAVorite GAMes to loosen
MY creative limbs is to MAKe A SHAPe
or A squiggle on a PAGe. TAKe A JUicy
Pen and use the next PAGe, or Blank
PAPer, to let the pen play.
Then, look AT the SHAPe very quickly,
and let the First thing THAT you see,
BeCOMe what it is!

MAKE A SHAPE or SQUIGGLE. let it reveAL
itseLF. ADD whATever lines Are necessAry
to MAKE it Known. Then write the naMe
UNDer the sHApe.

The squiggles and shapes I made resulted in SARK - the cartoon - which ran on Sundays for six years in the San Francisco Chronicle/Examiner.
Later, I developed SARK's San Francisco - my drawings of my love affair with this city.

remember to share your vision of the world. There is only one of you.

YOU ARE AMAZING

- - - - - - - - - - - - - -
Your creativity is limitless...

Most creativity is playing. Some of the best creative results come from "mistakes."

Here are some of my "mistakes":

Cutting: take a scissors and simply cut out the part you don't like!

Rubbing: smear everything together and see what happens.

Ripping: tear the painting into pieces, and use the pieces to make a new one.

Throwing: throw everything away and start over.

Combining: Add painting to your dancing, drawing to your singing.

PAy Attention to what you like.
TRust your HeARt and eyes.
Many people SAy "I Don't KnoW GooD
ARt From BAD."
WHATever you Like is GooD.

let's return to the creAtive iDeA or
DreAM you wrote Down in the
BeGinninG oF the BooK.

WHAT SMAll step or MicroMovement
Are you planninG to tAke? MAke it
a tiny step and write it Down.

USe this PAGe to list 5 wonderful
things that could HAppen if you let
your Dream come true. Be As wild and
Hopeful as your Dreams Are.

_ _ _ _ _ _ _ _ _ _ _ _ _

All your DreAms Are AlreaDY
      comiNG   TrUe

Where are your censors, negative judgements? Are you familiar with them now? They are like a player piano – they'll play any tape you put in – or just close the door, and you don't need to listen to their music.

Another marvelous book is called Spinning Inward by Maureen Murdock. It works with guided imagery and creativity. This exercise clears your mind!

The House of Perception

In this exercise, imagine going into the "room" of each sense – sight, hearing, smell, taste and touch – and cleaning out any cobwebs in each imaginary room that may be preventing you from perceiving each sense clearly.

Close your eyes and follow your breath
in... and... out... of your nostrils. Allow
your body to become very relaxed and
quiet as you breath in... and... out...
Now imagine that you are walking
down a street and you see a very interesting
House: this is the House of perception,
the House of your senses, and as you
walk into the House you see that There
Are many rooms with doors with symbols
on them.

The First room you come to has a large
eye on the door. You open the door and
realize that This is the room of vision.
It is filled with junk, The garbage
that you have put there over The years
to prevent you from seeing as clearly
as you might. In your mind's eye, see
all the junk and cobwebs in the room,
and begin to clean out The room of

Vision with cleansers, A Broom, A VACUUM — WHATever you need. (PAUSE one Minute)

When you Have FinisHeD, throw All The JunK out, open the windows, and let the room Fill with FresH Air. See it Bright and SHining. LooK out the window and see the scene outside, noticing All of the colors. (PAUSE 30 seconds)

now it is time to leave the room of vision.

min

Proceed now to the room of Hearing. it HAs A BiG eAr on the Door. As you open the door, you Hear a cacophony of discordant sounds. The room is Filled with rUBBisH. There is A lot of wool on the walls and A thick covering of wax all over the place.

Clean up the room of Hearing, MAKING
it As clean As you can, knowing you Are
improving The quality of Your Hearing.
(pAuse)
When you Have Finished with this
cleaning, open The windows and let
some Fresh air swoosh in. Hear it
swoosh in. Listen to The Breeze As
it whispers pAst you. (pAuse) now
listen closely to All The sounds Around
you (pAuse 30 seconds) listen to your
Breath (pAuse) and now it's time to
leave The room of Hearing.

Proceed now to the room of smell.
You know The room of smell Because
there is a large nose on The Door.
As you open The Door, you smell A
Combination of terrible scents,
including OLD MOLDY FOOD. Begin to
clean the room of smell, really

47

scrubbing all the corners and cracks in the room. Make it light and clean and sweet smelling. As you do so, you begin to smell all your favorite scents. (pause) enjoy this room now, breathing in it's fragrance deeply (pause 30 seconds) now it's time to leave the room of smell.

Proceed now to the room of touch, which has a large hand on the door. Clean it very thoroughly, throwing out all the junk that prevents you from feeling textures. (pause) When you've finished cleaning, move about the room and slowly feel the textured walls. rub your hands over the wallpaper, which is a mixture of velvet, silk, sandpaper, satin, ice and tree bark. notice how good everything feels to your skin. (pause 30 seconds) it is now time to leave the room of touch, and when you open your eyes you may want to touch the textures around you.

There is one more room to clean, and this room is the attic. You WALK up an OLD spiral staircase to the attic, which is full of COBWEBS and BATS. This is the room of your sixth sense... The room of extrasensory perception... The room of inner vision. and it is very dusty because it has not been used for a long time. you begin to clean the room of the sixth sense, and you notice a circular window at the far end of the room. it is so dirty that you cannot see out of it. you begin to scrape and wash it clean, and as you do so, a beautiful scene unfolds for you.

As you continue to look out this circular window, you notice All the colors sounds, smells, tastes and textures About this scene. (pAuse 30 seconds) it is now time to leave the room of the sixth sense. You close the door, wALK Down The spirAL stAircAse... pAst the rooms of your five senses and you leave your cleaning MAteriALs in the HAll closet. you leave the House of Perception and FinD yourseLF sitting Here.

I wanted this Book to be non-linear — to be opened anywhere and eAten From — Like ripe Fruit. I Frequently open Books At random, just to see WHAt They sAy. Try This now.
At the Age of 24, I MADe A DrAMAtic Decision. To Be creAtively ALive,

no Matter what. THis BOOK HAS
emerged From the living oF that Choice.
and yes, I "starved" For years BeFore
I Began to Heal From My BelieF in
SCArcity or selF Blame. Best BOOK
I've seen ABout this suBJect:
CreAting Money By Sanaya roman
and Dvane PACker.

People Frequently say to Me "you're
svcH A Free spirit!"
Arent spirits MADe to Be Free?
we Are All Free spirits.
We MUst cHoose to prActice FreeDoM.

- - - - - - - - - - -

Y o u   A r e   n o w   F r e e

WHAT'S HELPED FREE MY CREATIVE SPIRIT?

☆ BELIEF IN MIRACLES: experience, practice
  (you are always on your way to a miracle!)

☆ VISUALIZATION: imagery in my mind. Writing
  or drawing a picture of what I want.
  (I drew a picture of a "MAGIC COTTAGE" with
   a garden, and 2 weeks later, I moved in!)

☆ relaxation: stretching, napping, dreaming

☆ AFFIRMATION: positive, supportive thoughts
  contributing to self love.

☆ serenity: spiritual practice. HEALING.
           (belief in other than the self)

☆ support system: A circle of FABULOUS,
  talented, funny, loving friends and
  FAMILY. Both family of choice and of
  origin.

☆ reading: pleasure reading especially.

☆ HABIT OF COMPLETION: frees me to do more!

One of my Best Friends WAS Also
A Mentor. I recommend Mentors.
  Her name WAS MiRiAM WorNUM.
SHe DieD After 91 succulent years
oF writing, painting, creating, inhaling
LiFe. A photograph of Her FACe is
on the cover oF A wonderful Book
CAlled <u>crone</u> By BArBara WALKer.
  MiriAM WAS WiLD anD CrABBY,
sometimes Brittle, anD SHe WASn't
even 5 Feet HIGH. We TALKeD ABOUT
everything.
  SHe SHoweD Me Fierce creative pAssion
Burning constantly. Her BODY WAS an
AGeD Container- Her MinD viBrantly
Free.

        c r e A t i v e   s p i R i t s
        A r e   t r u l y   A G e l e s s

Try to FinD an OLD person. SpenD time there. I Dare you.

HOW TO TreAsure
an OLD person

Seek out OLD people. When You FIND SOME,
Give them Joy. listen closely. Develop Your
PAtience. Tune up Your sensitive Humor.
CRACK Your shell. remember that eACH
OLD person is A library. listen closely. GO
For A slow WALK in A SUNNY PARK. Be use·Full.
Bring the Gift of Your SeLf. Try enchantment.
Be Voluntary. Visit with MAGic. invent A
new Activity. Try playing their GAME.
let wisdom seep in. cradle Your own Future
OLD person. HUG willingly. Sew on A Button.
HandWrite A letter. TAKe A MIDNIGHT cruise
in A convertiBle. Try respect. Bestow surprise
GiFTS. Handle with CARiNG. Be Gentle.
MAKe A nourishing SouP. Believe in really
Living. PRAY together. GAMBle on love.
Plant A Tree in Honor of Your FriendshiP.
Plan something outrageous. embrace DeAth.
HOLD Hands AT TWiLiGHT. BAKe HilArious
cookies. listen closely. PAY Attention
To an OLD person.

THe TreAsures will Be revealed

♥ ©SARK '90

J U S T   F o r   o n e   D A Y

·〰·

C Heer up every person you interact with. (incluDinG yourselF)

HUG A Tree.
(note: the secret to HUGGinG Trees is to close your eyes so you Don't FeeL SHy. IF you HUG A Tree lonG enouGH, it will HUG you BACK!)

e AT A Banana popsicle, run through the sprinkler, lie on your BACK anD WATCH clouDs.

Be relentlessly positive.

THe worLD is crAvinG More creAtive Free spirits !

- - - - - - - - - - - - - - - -

Your imAGinat ion is wiDe anD Deep

Search your dearest friends and books (some of my best friends are books) for words of wisdom to sustain you.
Here are some of my favorites. Cut them out and put them up on mirrors, walls, or your T.V.

— — — — — — — — — — — — — —

"When I have something to say that is too difficult for adults, I write for children. They have not closed the shutters. They like it when you rock the boat."

Madeleine L'Engle

— — — — — — — — — — — — — —

A non-creative environment is one that constantly bombards us, I said, overloads our switchboard with noise, with agitation and with visual stimuli. Once we can detach ourselves from all these distractions, find a way of "inscape" of "centering," the same environment becomes creative again.

Frederick Franck

"AT FIRST people refuse to believe that A strange new thing can be done, and then they begin to hope it can be done, then they see it can be done — then it is done and all the world wonders why it was not done centuries ago."

Frances Hodgson Burnett

"if you stuff yourself full of poems, essays, plays, stories, novels, films comic strips, magazines, music, you automatically explode every morning like old Faithful. I have never had a dry spell in my life, mainly because I feed myself well, to the point of bursting. I wake early and hear my morning voices leaping around in my head like jumping beans. I get out of bed to trap them before they escape."

Ray Bradbury

"You need only claim the events of your life to make yourself yours. When you truly possess all you have been and done, which may take some time, you are fierce with reality."

Florida Scott Maxwell

57

CREATIVITY ADORES SOLITUDE.

PROVIDE QUIET CREATIVE TIME FOR YOUR-
SELF. IT CAN FIRST FIT INTO THE CRACKS
OF YOUR LIFE, AND AS YOU NURTURE IT,
IT WILL EXPAND INTO A GLORIOUS INTERIOR
GARDEN.

I LIVE IN A WORLD OF BOOKS.

I HAVE AN ASTOUNDING APPETITE FOR
BOOKS, AND LEARNED TO READ VERY FAST.
IT IS COMMON FOR ME TO READ A BOOK
OR TWO A DAY.

SO, I WILL SHARE SOME BOOKS THAT
ARE DEAR TO ME, AND HAVE HELPED
MY CREATIVE SPIRIT.

SHORT succulent BOOK LIST

JOURNAL OF A SOLITUDE BY MAY SARTON

PAINT AS YOU LIKE AND DIE HAPPY BY Henry Miller

Mr. BASS and the MUSHroom PLANET BY eleanor CAMEron

GIFTS FROM the SEA BY anne Morrow LindBergh

MY FAMILY and other animals BY GERALD DURRELL

TRACKS BY RoByn DAVIDSon

IN MY own WAY BY ALan WATTS

EARTHLY PARADISE BY COLette

Writing Down the Bones BY NAtalie GoLdBerg

WISDOM OF the HeARt BY Henry Miller

59

MY FAVORITE PLACE TO READ BOOKS AS A CHILD (BESIDES MY BED) WAS IN THE ROUGH SAFETY OF THE APPLE TREE BRANCHES IN MY BACKYARD.

REMEMBER WHEN THE WHOLE WORLD WAS THE TREE YOU WERE CLIMBING?

SOME MORE MARVELOUS BOOKS

WILD MIND BY NATALIE GOLDBERG

THE ZEN OF SEEING BY FREDERICK FRANCK

LOVE IS LETTING GO OF FEAR BY GERALD JAMPOLSKY

DON'T PUSH THE RIVER IT FLOWS BY ITSELF BY BARRY STEVENS

GONE AWAY LAKE BY ELIZABETH ENRIGHT

HEALING THE SHAME THAT BINDS YOU BY JOHN BRADSHAW

YOU CAN HEAL YOUR LIFE BY LOUISE HAY

HAROLD AND THE PURPLE CRAYON BY CROCKETT JOHNSON

HOME COMING BY JOHN BRADSHAW

STAND STILL LIKE THE HUMMINGBIRD BY HENRY MILLER

MAX MAKES A MILLION BY MAIRA KALMAN

62

WHAT DID others tell you when you tried to DRAW, paint, Dance, sing, or create something new? These Are opinions of others FroM years pAst. Write Down a MeMory you HAVe of BeinG tolD something like this:

now, transforM tHAt MeMory.
Here was one oF Mine:
"you're not reAlly A writer."
Use the langUage FroM the MeMory, and rewrite it.
"OH yes I AM! I AM reAlly A writer."

MeMory:

transforMAtion:

You Are now Free FroM the pAst

WHen ALBerT WiGGAM, AutHor oF <u>explore your MiND</u> WAS ASKeD iF lAcK oF ABility CAUSeD Most FAilures, he SAiD "No. FeAr DoeS. it DeFeATS More people than poverty, iGnorance, superstition, ill HeAlth and lAcK oF Mental ABility."

aND AS For rejection?
iF you're not BeiNG rejecteD, you're not reAcHiNG FAr enough!

In My clASS, "Art aND aDventures with SARK" I took 4 eleven year olDS to A Fancy Hotel with GlASS elevAtors, to "DrAw the city From ABove." unexpecteDly, the GirlS BecAMe SHy aND reluctant, SAyiNG,
"But what iF people Get in the elevAtor?"

I MARCHED into the elevator and SAID "Well then, we'll DRAW their SHOES!" Which we DID. It resulted in A Hilarious Afternoon of DRAWING people's shoes, pretending not to speak english. We must surround ourselves and our CHILDren with free creativity — in thought and spirit.

"We need to trust CHILDren From A very early Age with independent study, perHAps Arranged in school BUt taking place AWAy From the institutional setting. Independent study, community service Done on "school time," ADventures in experience, lArge Doses of privacy and solitude, A thousand Different Apprenticeships in the working world."

                    JOHN GAtto
        new york city "Teacher of The year"

When I was young, and desperate to escape family dysfunctions, my only free creative time was at night.

"I'm a reader, a writer, a child who won't go to bed at night. I stay in my room, reading and reading some more. By crack of the door light, flashlight, nightlight, moonlight but almost never the light in my room. My father took all the lamps out of my room, for fear I would never sleep! I said, "sleep is fine, even sublime–in the daytime, but not at night time, cause that's the best time!"

I saved up bread from dinner, rolled it into little balls and balanced them on my nightlight, cooking them there. They tasted toasty and sweet. Delicious things happened at night...

Doorbells Glowed, Rhubarb Beckoned, Grass
Grew extra Green and Juicy. The World
Felt Dark and secret. It was when the
Stairs creaked loudest. Comic Books and
Poems, A list of Dirty words, Moonbaths
in Bed. No rules! The Air was Full of
the Dreams of the sleeping people."

excerpted from A work in progress

"Just mere thoughts—Are As Powerful
As electric Batteries—As Good For one
As sunlight is, or As Bad For one As
Poison. To let A Sad thought or A Bad
one Get into your mind is As Dangerous
As letting A scarlet fever Germ Get
into your Body. If you let it stay there
After it HAS Got in you may never
Get over it As long As you Live."

Frances Hodgson Burnett

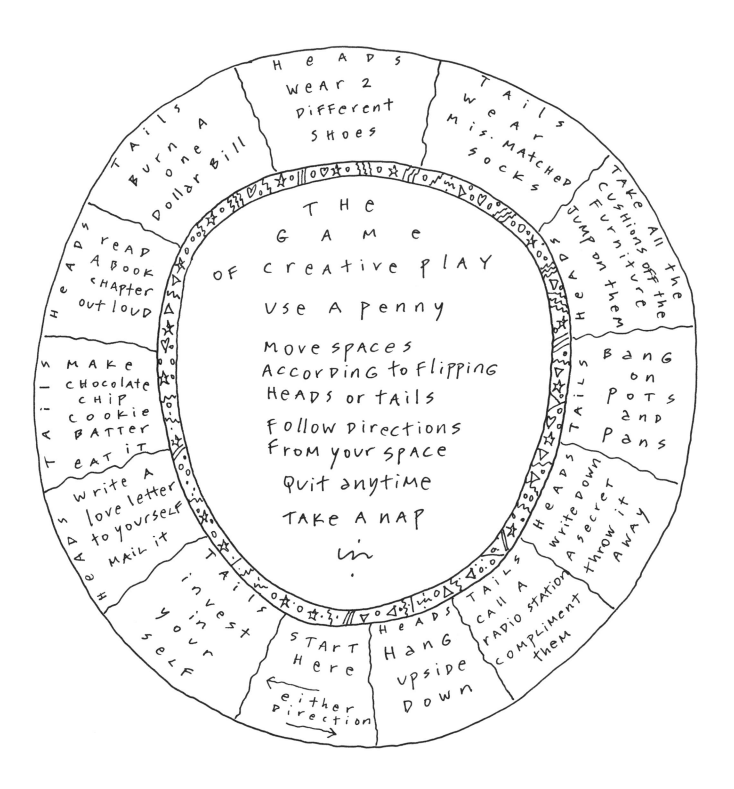

THE GAME
OF creative pLAY

USE A penny

MOVE SPACES
ACCORDING to FLiPPING
HEADS or tAILS

FOLLOW Directions
FROM your SPACE

QUit anytime

TAKE A NAP

HEADS
weAr 2
DiFFerent
SHoes

TAILS
weAr
miS.MATCHeD
SoCKS

TAKE ALL the CUSHioNS oFF the FurNiture JUMP oN them — HEADS

BAnG oN PoTS anD PaNS — TAILS

HEADS write Down A secret throw it AWAY

cALL A radio station compliment them — TAILS

HanG upSide DowN — HEADS

TAIls invest in your SELF

write A love letter to yourself — MAIL it — HEADS

MAKE CHocolate CHIP cookie BATTER eAT iT — TAILS

HEADS reAD A Book cHApter out louD

TAiLs BurN A oNe Dollar Bill

START Here ← either Direction →

"if you are doing something you would do for nothing - then you are on your way to salvation. And if you could drop it in a minute and forget the outcome, you are even further along. And if while you are doing it you are transported into another existence, there is no need for you to worry about the future."

Dr. George Sheehan

THIS is FOR YOU:

uncover your DREAMS

open the treasure chests

SHAKE OFF the DUST

expose your creative FILM
to the light

Try this. Write a portrait or Description of your "ideal self." Make it glow. reveal all your best qualities. start with I am...

YOU
Are
rAre
anD
WOnDerOUS

Give yourself and others GIFTS!
Gifts can be small treasures that are
absolutely free. Leaves, dried flowers,
fruit, tiny rocks, pine cones. Serenade
a friend. Write a love note on the side-
WALK with colored CHALK. MAKE A SMALL
Xeroxed Book of poems you've written.
Have a private dance recital at a park—
invite a friend. Have a picnic with only
desserts. MAKE A PAPER DOLL OF A loved
one, with clothes. Invent a new GAME,
and play it with someone you love. WASH
Someone else's HAIR. Trade clothes.
MAKE A Diorama with A SHOE BOX.

When I used to ask My Mother so
Plaintively "But there's nothin to do!"
SHe would reply
"You could DIG A Hole to China."
and just for an instant, I was
transported...

IMAGINE your "creative companion."
WHAT Does it look like? animal or Human?
Physical or spirit? PAst or present?
With you All the time, or sometimes?

· um ·

One of my Best creative companions is A
Black cat named Jupiter. He eats Paper
and Discovers treasures. In Fact, He
is responsible for the publication of
my poster: How to Be an Artist. every
Day, I WOULD WAKe up to Him carefully
Peeling the poster off the WALL and
Putting it on my Bed. Finally, I sHAReD
it with more people, and the orders
Flooped in. Sometimes I tell this
Story when People Ask why I FeeD
Jupiter "Gourmet" CAT FOOD AT 79¢
A can! Jupiter is Also known As
the "yes cat" BeCAUSe He Lives in
Such A positive world.

"THE THING is to BECOME
A MASTER anD in your OLD
AGE to ACQuire the COUrAGE
to Do what CHILDren DiD
when they Knew nothinG."

Henry Miller

- - - - - - - - - - - - - -

"One of the important thinGs
I learneD in MAKinG wAtercolors
wAs not to worry, not to cAre
too MUCH."

Henry Miller

- - - - - - - - - - - - - -

"TO HAVe FAith, to Give, anD to
prAy thAT The results will Be
GooD. every potentiAL ARTiST
SHoULD HAVe A CHance."

Henry Miller

Henry Miller Gave me the name SARK.
He HAD DieD, and CAMe into My DreAM
to SAy,
"your name will Be SARK, and your
ARtwork will Be FAMOUS BeFore your
writing."
I woke up and thought, "IM not Going
to Be SARK - ThAt's an ODD name." AND
I wrote the DreAM DOWN in my JOURNAL.
Two weeks later, Henry WAS BACK in
another DreAM. This time He SAiD,
"your name will Be SUsan ArieL RainBow
Kennedy."
since My name was AlreADy Susan
Kennedy, I thought it woulD Be
wonDerFul to ADD ArieL RainBow,
anD So I went to court to MAKe it
leGAL. AS I SAT there, DOODLinG on
A piece of paper in court, I reAlizeD
it spelleD SARK !

A message to you:
Go now.

Your creative spirit is free.
Write to me. Send me something
from your heart.

STAMP
of
Approval

TO: SARK
c/o Celestial Arts
PO Box 7327
Berkeley CA 94707

A GARDEN OF FRIENDS BlOOMING

SARK

78

THE BIG THANK YOU PAGE ♡

MY CREATIVE LIFE HAS BEEN SUPPORTED, GUIDED, ENCOURAGED AND CELEBRATED BY THE FOLLOWING PEOPLE, ANIMALS, PLACES AND THINGS.

love, SARK
the MAGIC COTTAGE, SAN FRANCISCO
JULY 1 1991

ALL THANKS TO:

MY PARENTS, MARJE AND ARTHUR ♡ MY BROTHER ANDREW ☆
DAVID E. EARLY ☆ Helen Grieco ♡ MiriAM Wornum ☆ Jupiter ☆
LARRY A. ROSENTHAL ♡ AMEUR BEN ARAB ♡ SUSAN BEARDSLEY ☆
PARADISE ISLAND ☆ Julie ELiZABeth evans ☆ TeleGRAPH Hill ♡
ROBIN AND JOHN ♡ Henry Miller ☆ New York City ♡ Emily claire ☆
Deidre SOMMERS ☆ OX FAMILY ♡ CAFE MARTiniQue ☆ GiBi ♡
JOANN DECK ♡ Lisa FlanaGan ☆ BOPPA ♡ WHITE BEAR LAKE ☆
Luella ♡ SARAH HANSON ☆ CHRISTina Merwin @ rose Frances ♡
MicHael Bell ☆ roBert Brewer Hamilton youNG ♡ Nanew & Marcus ☆
RiCK Silverstein ♡ Jessie & JiM ☆ CeciLiA AND Lulu ♡ MANDALAY ♡
The Filbert steps ☆ Susan Harrow ♡ The word Yes ☆ GODDesses ☆
ADRienne AND Ken ♡ All telepHones ☆ MARY AND George ♡ GOD ☆
ANGels ☆ everyBODY At the ReD Rose ♡ My Dreams ☆ San Francisco ♡
All puBlic liBraries... AND to the Henry Miller Memorial LiBrary ☆

AND NOW, TO YOU! _____
your name ♡

DeliGHTFully, SARK

A very special thanks to CelestiAL ARTS AND the outstanding JOANN DECK ☆

79

Sources

PAGE 6. De Mille, Agnes & Graham, Martha. *Dance to the Piper*. Boston, MA: Little, Brown & Company, 1951.

15. Lang, Doe. *The Charisma Book*. Ridgefield, CT: Wyden Books, 1980.

44. Murdock, Maureen. *Spinning Inward*. Boston, MA: Shambhala, 1987.

56. L'Engle, Madeleine. From a talk given at Grace Cathedral in San Francisco, 1987.

56. Franck, Frederick. *The Zen of Seeing*. New York: Vintage Books, 1973.

57. Burnett, Frances Hodgson. *The Secret Garden*. New York: Dell Publishing, 1986.

57. Bradbury, Ray. From an Article in *Writer's Digest*, February 1991.

57. Maxwell, Florida Scott. *The Measure of My Days*. New York: Penguin Books, 1972.

65. Gatto, John. From an Article by Bill Mandel in the *San Francisco Examiner*, June 1990.

69. Sheehan, George. *Personal Best*. Emmaus, PA: Rodale Press, 1989.

75. Miller, Henry. *The Angel is my Watermark*. New York: Henry N. Abrams, 1962. *My Life and Times*. New York: Gemini Smith Inc./ Playboy Press, 1971. *Remember to Remember*. New York: New Directions, 1967.

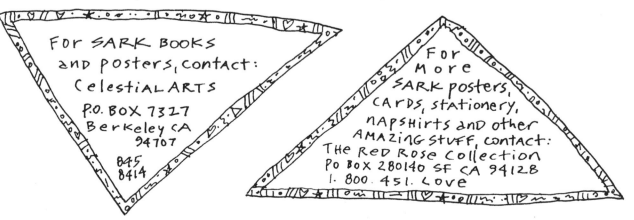

For SARK books and posters, contact:
Celestial Arts
P.O. Box 7327
Berkeley CA
94707
845 8414

For More SARK posters, cards, stationery, napshirts and other amazing stuff, contact:
The Red Rose Collection
PO Box 280140 SF CA 94128
1.800.451.Love